Uncle

CC & Me

PART II

D0864150

Uncle CC & Me

PART II

Rhonda Dula

atmosphere press

© 2022 Rhonda Dula

Published by Atmosphere Press

Cover design by Ronaldo Alves

No part of this book may be reproduced without permission from the author except in brief quotations and in reviews.

atmospherepress.com

DEDICATED TO:

Deniseea Michelle &
Her Great Commission 5-G Ministry:

1. Christopher
2. LaSean
3. DeJa
4. Olivia
5. Orlando Jr.

1. Teacher = Grounded
(Teaches true word & solid basic
instructional foundations)

2. Pastor = Guardians
(Protective order and/or protective watch)

3. Evangelist = Gathers
(Brings flocks together)

4. Prophet = Guide
(Directs how to proceed)

5. Apostle = Govern
(Established authority and/or determined control)

"GREAT COMMISSION," making of DISCIPLESHIP —
Do what "HE" has done in us and with us Saints as we
pass it forward throughout the world,
making leaders today for tomorrow's future!

Chapter 1

THE REASSIGNMENT –
U.S. Marine Corps Air Station

El Toro USMC Base, Southern California – 1964

Marine Corps Air Station El Toro was a United States Marine Corps Air Station located near Irvine, California. Before it was decommissioned in 1999, it was the 4,682-acre (19 km²) home of Marine Corps aviation on the West Coast. Designated as a Master Jet Station, its four runways (two of 8,000 feet (2,400 m) and two of 10,000 feet (3,000 m)) could handle the largest aircraft in the U.S. military inventory. While it was active, all U.S. Presidents in the post-World War II era landed in Air Force One at this airfield. The El Toro "Flying Bull" was designed by Walt Disney Studios in 1944. It survived virtually unchanged until the close of the Air Station in 1999.

The land area originally taken by the air station is planned to be converted into a large recreational center, the Orange County Great Park. The site is currently used as a filming location and was the set of the test track for

3

the United States' version of the *Top Gear* franchise.

In May of 1942, Lieutenant Colonel William Fox was directed to select the sites for all of the Marine Corps' West Coast air stations. Fox sought the most expeditious and low-cost option and thus chose the already existing airports of El Centro, Mojave, and Santa Barbara. For the fourth station, he chose land that had previously been looked at by the Navy for a blimp base. The Marine Corps gave the owner of the land—a farmer named James Irvine Sr.—$100,000 for 4,000 acres (20 km²), including 1,600 acres (6.5 km²) designated for a blimp base. Construction of MCAS El Toro began on August 3, 1942 on land previously owned by the Irvine Company. The company greatly resisted the station's construction at this site, which at the time contained the largest lima bean field in North America, which was the company's prime source of revenue; the name *El Toro* came from the nearby small community which in 1940 only had a population of 130 people.

The base headquarters was established on November 4, 1942, and the first landing occurred in late November when Major Michael Carmichael, flying from Camp Kearny, was forced to make an emergency landing among the construction equipment. January 1943 saw the first operational units arriving at MCAS El Toro. First aboard were Marine Base Defense Aircraft Group 41 and VMF-113. They were followed later in the month by VMSB-142, VMF-224, VMSB-231, and VMSB-232, who were returning from fighting during the Battle of Guadalcanal in order to re-organize, re-equip, and train. Soon after its opening, El Toro was handling the largest tactical aerodrome traffic on the Pacific Coast.

Already the largest Marine air station on the West Coast, in 1944 funds were approved to double its size and operations. By the end of 1944, the base would be home to 1,248 officers and 6,831 enlisted personnel.

In 1950, El Toro was selected as a permanent Master Jet Station for the Fleet Marine Forces, Pacific; to support this new role, the aviation infrastructure at El Toro was again expanded significantly. For most of the ensuing years, El Toro served as the primary base for Marine Corps west coast fighter squadrons. During the 1960s, many U.S. Marines left for and returned from Vietnam at El Toro MCAS. In 1958, Marine Corps Air Station Miami was closed, which brought the third Marine Aircraft Wing to El Toro.

During the presidency of Richard M. Nixon, MCAS El Toro was used for flights to and from his "Western White House" in San Clemente, California.

The land originally surrounding the base was mostly of agricultural use when it first opened, but in the late 1980s and early 1990s, residential development started to begin in the area; most of it was directly in the path of the base's runways, which proved to be a major problem as the constant loud noise produced by jets and helicopters passing overhead was very irritating to those living in the area. Few desired to move there because of this, causing the new neighborhoods to struggle.

1993 – MCAS El Toro was designated for closing by the Base Realignment and Closure Commission, and all of its activities were to be transferred to Marine Corps Air Station Miramar. The station officially closed on July 2, 1999.

C O D E   O F   E T H I C S
(COE)

"Difference is that raw and powerful connection from which our personal power is forged."

Integrity and ethics exist in the individual or they do not exist at all. They must be upheld by individuals or they are not upheld at all. In order for integrity and ethics to be within our characteristics, we must strive to be:

- Honest and trustworthy in all our relationships

- Reliable in carrying out tasks and responsibilities

- Truthful and accurate in what we say & do

- Cooperative & constructive in all tasks & undertakings

- Fair/considerate in our treatment of all fellow persons

- Economical in utilizing all our resources

- Dedicated in services to ourselves and others to improve the quality of life in the world in which we live

Integrity and high standards of ethics require hard work, courage, and major choices. Consultation between individuals will be necessary to determine a proper course of action. Integrity and ethics may sometimes require us to sacrifice our own individual opportunities. In the long run, however, we will be better served by doing what is right rather than what is expedient.

Orange County, California – El Toro (USMC)
U.S. Military Station Location

Orange County, California was known for the many, many orange groves located throughout the cities within. Orange County was located south of Los Angeles County, north of San Diego County, northeast of San Bernardino County, and southeast of Riverside County.

Yvette Raymar came to Southern California when her father, Colonel CJ Jackson, was sent on a military reassignment to settle in Orange County at El Toro (USMC) Marine Air Base, where she first met Uncle CC—aka the famous U.S. Agricultural Labor Worker's activist, Mr. César Chavez. In 1964, she knew him as Uncle CC.

César Chavez was an American labor leader and civil rights activist who founded the National Farm Workers Association in 1962. Originally a Mexican-American farm worker, Chavez became the best-known Latino-American civil rights activist and was strongly promoted by the American labor. César Chavez led the United Farm Workers of America and saw its share of defeats, but also its many historic victories. Under César , the UFW achieved unprecedented gains for farm workers. Among them were the first genuine collective bargaining agreements between farm workers and growers in American history.

2 Corinth 4:13 – *And since we have the same spirit of faith; According to what is written, "I believed and therefore I spoke," we also believe and therefore speak. Every believer has been given the same measure of faith. In order to see the promises of God come to pass in your life of God. As you give your faith a voice, you will see God's promises come to pass.*

1 Corinth 13:13 – *Three things will last forever—faith, hope, and the greatest of these is love...*

Colossians 3:23 – *Whatever you do, work with all your heart, as working for the Lord, not for human masters...*

The scripture talks about believers representing God here on the earth. We are Christ's ambassadors. If we're to represent God properly, we should do it with joy, with enthusiasm, with a smile. People of faith may not want to listen to what we believe, but they certainly watch how we live. We are living epistles read by all. Some may not read the Bible, but they're reading our lives. Preach at all times; use words only when necessary...you have to give expression to that faith through the words that you speak. That's why the Scripture tells us, "Let the weak say, "I am strong" –not the opposite. "I am so tired, I am so rundown." That's calling in the wrong things. Let the poor say, "I am well off"—not, "I am in debt." When you give your faith a voice, when you start speaking the promises of God, the Bible says that He watches over His Word to bring it to pass in your life. The key is that we can't allow words to defeat or negativity to come out of our mouths...

CHARACTER PROFILE

Responsive – Character leads, manages, and coordinates the natural response to acts of professional development, health, and wellness.

Preventive – Character detects, deters, and mitigates health and wellness through character awareness.

Protective – Safeguard your health and risk critical threats to your lifestyle. Develop acts of management to your natural health risk and other potential acts of weaknesses.

Awareness – Achieve effectiveness and operational synergies through leadership education. Create professional development, promote universal awareness, present with applied organizational leadership. Set strategic goals, mission objectives, and visions to support spiritual leadership character.

Values – Most important leadership quality is through leadership of character: to create a culture that promotes health, fitness, wellness, and teamwork to achieve lifestyle development and management of objective values. Values serve effectively by facilitating professional and personal leadership management and development.

Organization – Character leads to unity, efforts to restore good services, and rebuilds community acts of organizational values. Objective organization is developed through the value of character building.

Acknowledgment – Act on our character gifts. We all have it; it is the creative power within. Embrace it. Acknowledgment it. Give permission to use it. It is our divine right.

"P O W E R   P R A Y E R!"

POWER IS PRAYER*PRAYER IS POWER
****

THE VALUE OF TIME IS THE VALUE OF LIFE**********
HOW VALUABLE IS YOUR TIME TODAY?????????????
HOW DO YOU VALUE EACH DAY?????????????
HOW DO YOU VALUE EACH MOMENT?????????????
HOW DO YOU VALUE EACH HOUR?????????
HOW DO YOU VALUE EACH MINUTE?????????

The Individual Who Kneels To God Can Stand Up To Anything...But now, O Lord, You are our Savior; We are the clay, And You our potter; And all we are the Work of Your Hands...

WHEN WE ARE PRAYING FOR OTHERS:

Life-affirming words and thoughts of others are prayers reaching out to bless the body of "Christ" in positive ways. No matter what others are going through, support the body of "Christ" in prayer. Affirmations of Truth are the foundation of prayers. The power release through affirmations establishes "Truth" in our consciousness. Consciousness of others enters into the "Presence in Prayer." We embrace others, near and far. Hold "Others" in our hearts and in our thoughts, affirming in "Divine Order" through our power of prayer...

In 1946, César E. Chávez joined the U.S. Navy and served in the Pacific after WWII as a seaman, returning in 1948. "He belonged to generations of Latinos who returned from service after WWII, Korea, Vietnam.

César E. Chávez was awarded the Presidential Medal of Freedom. His occupation(s) were as follows: Military Navy Veteran, Labor Leader, and Civil Rights Activist. Born in Yuma, Arizona, USA. Died in 1993.

A PRAYER FOR RESTORATION:

"We must live with a repentant heart, our mind is renewed! We want our thoughts to be truthful, we want our ways to be true and loving in all our ways... Please forgive us of anger, forgive us of all that we have done wrong against heaven. Please forgive them who harbor unforgiving hearts against heaven. We release anger, frustration, and confusion. We replace it with the compassion of love, which flows from our heart and we will continue to have love for others, we know that forgiveness relieves pain, confess this to be true in the name of fellowship for humanity from this day forward. We let it go now and forever! We give it all to the heavens. We pray that fear will no longer hold us hostage" FEAR is: False Evidence Appearing Real... They Will Soar On Wings Like Eagles. (Isaiah 40:31) God's Promise To Us Is...Strength

***

César E. Chávez was a good man who dedicated his life to helping others. César was born to parents who taught him important ideas about hard work, education, and respect. As a young boy, César worked on his family's farm feeding and watering the animals, collecting eggs, and bringing water to the house.

César's parents thought school was important. School was hard for César because the teachers only spoke English and César did not understand English. César thought some teachers were mean because they would punish him when he spoke Spanish. César learned to read English in school and he learned to read Spanish from his uncles.

César's parents were very strict and taught him and his sisters and brothers to show respect to others.

His parents also taught him that it was important to help others. César and his family often helped his uncles, aunts, and cousins by giving them food when they had little to eat.

When César was ten years old, his family's home was taken away from them because they did not have enough money.

César's family moved to California to find work. They began working on farms, picking fruits and vegetables. César's family would move from farm to farm looking for work, just like many other families who also lost their homes.

César's family moved often. Moving did not bother César or his sisters and brothers too much because their parents loved them and because they were always happy to be together as a family.

When César was a teenager, he and his older sister Rita would help other farm workers and neighbors by driving them to the hospital to see a doctor. Without their help, these people would have had a very difficult time getting a doctor's help.

The people César helped often wanted to give him a little bit of money to pay for gas and for his help. César never took any of their money because his mother would have been mad at him. She used to say, "You always have to help the needy, and God will help you."

A few years later, César volunteered to serve in the United States Navy. César, like many American men and women, served in the military to fight for freedom and to protect the people of the United States.

After two years in the Navy, César returned home and married his girlfriend, Helen. After a short time, they moved to San Jose, California and began a family.

Life changed for César when he met a man named Fred Ross. Fred Ross believed that if people worked together, they could make their community better. Fred Ross hired César to work for him in the Community Service Organization.

The Community Service Organization worked to help people. César now worked to bring people together to identify problems and find ways to solve their problems. Many problems were not solved because community leaders did not respect all people.

César, Fred Ross, and the Community Service Organization helped people in the community learn how to vote. They also taught people that community leaders respected voters. Community leaders worked harder to solve the problems of voters. César worked in many communities in California to help people gain the respect they deserved.

After helping many people gain the respect of community leaders, César left the Community Service Organization to help farm workers gain the respect and dignity they deserved.

César started the National Farm Worker Association to help improve the working conditions of farm workers. African Americans, Filipinos, white Americans, Mexican Americans and Mexicans, and men and women of all backgrounds joined César.

César did not believe in violence. Like Martin Luther King, César wanted to bring change in a nonviolent way. Many people came to help César. Many people supported César because he believed in nonviolence. Like César, they also believed that farm workers deserved better treatment, respect, dignity, justice, and fairness.

After five years, some growers in California agreed with César and started to provide farm workers with fresh water to drink, bathrooms, and better pay. César, the farm workers, and their friends won, making farm workers' lives better.

César dedicated the rest of his life to making the world a better place and to serving others. He continued to work to bring respect, dignity, justice, and fair treatment to the poor, to farm workers, and to people everywhere.

César died on April 23, 1993. He was sixty-six years old. People all over the world remember César E. Chávez as a man of courage who fought to improve the lives of all people.

Chapter 2

Caesar E. Chávez

--- *Good actions give strength to ourselves and inspire good actions in others.*

--- *A journey of 1,000 miles begins with a single step.*

--- *Character is like a tree and a reputation like a shadow. The shadow is what we think of it; the tree is the real thing.*

--- *Ability is what you're capable of doing motivation determines what you do. Attitude determines how well you do it!*

--- *Unless a man undertakes more than he possibly can do, he will never do all that he can...*

– César E. Chávez

INSPIRED BY HIS WORD!

When you are downcast and discouraged, read Psalm 37—the entire Psalm—because it is the voice of one who is in utter despair and totally broken. He gives us hope by reminding us that *"many are the afflictions of the righteous, but the Lord delivers him out of them all"* (Psalm 37:19). Notice that the Psalmist said, "Many are the afflictions of the righteous," and not just a few, and those who have had Jesus' righteousness imputed to them can stand before God as cleansed and having Jesus' righteousness (2 Corinth 5:21). So this Psalm is about us! Claim it, believe Him, and pour out your soul to Him. He is near you if you're brokenhearted and saves everyone who is crushed in spirit. More than that, He says He will deliver us out of all of our troubles, but only if we cry out to Him for help. Sometimes my pride gets in the way when I get in trouble and need help. That's too bad because God will resist me when I'm full of myself and will give me His grace only when I humble myself (James 4:6).

That's why I need to swallow my pride and cry out to Him for help because God not only hears our cries, He moves into action by delivering us from them all. He is very near to those who are brokenhearted and crushed in spirit. God delivers us out of our troubles, not just some but *all* of them, even though He doesn't give us a time frame for this deliverance. We have to trust Him. Our God is so faithful, even when we aren't.

Psalm 126:5-6— "Those who sow in tears shall reap with shouts of joy! He, who goes out weeping, bearing the seed for sowing, shall come home with shouts of joy, bringing his sheaves with him."

This Psalm reminds me of a farmer. They sow a seed and reap a crop, but it comes much later. So too for those who weep today, for they will surely reap with shouts of joy on the day of the Lord's visitation, and all of their suffering won't be able to compare with the glory they'll see on that great day (Rom 8:28). Even though today's sowing is hard, not one tear will be wasted in the glorious kingdom to come.

The Bible says that it's out of the abundance of the heart that the mouth speaks (Luke 6:45). If you're feeding your heart negative feelings, they're certain to end up coming out of your mouth and making the situation worse.

But when we're living in a place of daily gratitude for the things that God has given us, then, like a good father, He causes them to multiply in our lives!

Today, choose to live in gratitude, (PLACE YOUR OWN NAME HERE). Make it a life habit, begin and end each day with gratitude.

"He shall see his seed; he shall prolong his days, and the pleasure of the Lord shall prosper in his hand." Isaiah 53:10

I don't know about you, but sometimes things can rub me the wrong way...in other words, annoy or irritate me. How do I react when that happens?

I choose gratitude rather than an "attitude." I consciously try to choose to be thankful for all the good things that God has given me, rather than complaining!

Plead for the speedy fulfillment of this promise, all ye who love the Lord. It is easy work to pray when we are grounded and bottomed, as to our desires, upon God's own promise. How can He that gave the word refuse to keep it? Immutable veracity cannot demean itself by a lie, and eternal faithfulness cannot degrade itself by neglect. God must bless his SON; His covenant binds Him to it. That which the Spirit prompts us to ask for Jesus, is that which God decrees to give Him. Whenever you are praying for the kingdom of Christ, let your eyes behold the dawning of the blessed day which draws near, when the Crucified shall receive His coronation in the place where men rejected Him.

Have courage that you prayerfully work and toil for Christ with success of the very smallest kind—it shall not be so always; better times are before you. Your eyes cannot see the blissful future: borrow the telescope of faith; wipe the misty breath of your doubts from the glass; look through it and behold the coming glory. Reader, let us ask, do you make this your constant prayer? Remember that the same Christ who tells us to say, "Give us this day our daily bread," had first given us this petition, "Hallowed be thy name; Thy kingdom come; Thy will be done in earth as it is in heaven."

Let not your prayers be all concerning your own sins, your own wants, your own imperfections, your own trials, but let them climb the starry ladder and get up to Christ himself, and then, as you draw nigh to the blood-sprinkled mercy-seat, offer this prayer continually, "Lord, extend the kingdom of thy dear Son." Such a petition, fervently presented, will elevate the spirit of all your devotions. Mind that you prove the sincerity of your prayer by laboring to promote the Lord's glory.

"Lift up your head, fix your eyes on Me and walk, go forward, run, dance, and sing...I'm with you!"

I am the Lord who hears you...

I didn't miss your first cry, your first word, and your first breath. Each of your words rises to Me...I hear every one of your prayers.

I am the Lord who upholds you...

Each day, each hour, each moment, I am with you. I walk with you. I give you the strength to do the impossible. To move mountains and walk through each day with confidence.

I am the Lord with you...

Never think that you're alone, abandoned, or orphaned...I am the One who IS, and I am WITH you. I am FOR you.

Lift up your head, fix your eyes on Me and walk, go forward, run, dance, sing...I'm walking with you, I'm running with you, I live with you! I am with you! Be abundantly blessed! Psalm 121:5/Matthew 1:23

GIVE IT TO THE LORD

The Bible says to go to prayer and give it to the Lord. God has the strength to lift you up; to choose the path it takes; to lift the load that weighs you down. He'll help with all mistakes. His word is the way of freedom, His wine of love has been poured, and such peace will fill a weary heart when you give it to the Lord.

ALL TOGETHER NOW...APPLAUSE FOR GOD! SING SONGS TO THE TUNE OF GLORY. (PSALM 66:1)

There are three simple things you can do each day that will breathe new life into everything you do:

First, speak words of faith and victory out loud. As a child of the Most High God, you should have boldness when you declare, "I can do all things through Christ who strengthens me! My path is getting brighter and brighter."

Next, take time to write down the good things that God does for you each day. When you begin to look for HIS goodness, you will quickly discover that HE is working in your life.

Finally, be thankful. Take a moment every day to thank the Lord for all HE has done for you. When you develop a thankful heart, you are changing your focus from how big your problems are to how big your GOD is!

Summer 1964

July 2 – President Lyndon Johnson signs the Civil Rights Act of 1964 into law, abolishing racial segregation in the United States.

July 8 – U.S. military personnel announce that U.S. casualties in Vietnam have risen to 1,387, including 399 dead and 17 MIA.

July 10 – The Beatles return to Liverpool in triumph after their successful US tour, just in time for the premiere of their film *A Hard Day's Night*. This day is celebrated as Beatles Day in Liverpool, Hamburg, and other cities.

July 16 – At the Republican National Convention in San Francisco, U.S. presidential nominee Barry Goldwater declares that "extremism in the defense of liberty is no vice," and "moderation in the pursuit of justice is no virtue."

July 18 – Six days of race riots begin in Harlem.
– Judith Graham Pool publishes her discovery of cryoprecipitate, a frozen blood clotting product made from plasma primarily to treat hemophiliacs around the world.
– *False Hare* is the final Warner Bros. cartoon with "target" titles.

July 19 – Vietnam War: At a rally in Saigon, South Vietnamese Prime Minister Nguyen Khanh calls for expanding the war into North Vietnam.

July 20 – Vietnam War: Viet Cong forces attack a provincial capital, killing 11 South Vietnamese military personnel and 40 civilians (30 of which are children).
– The National Movement of the Revolution is instituted as the sole legal political party in the Republic of Congo.

July 22 – The second meeting of the Organization of African Unity is held.

July 23 – There is a minor criticality accident at a United Nuclear Corporation Fuels Recovery Plant in Wood River

Junction, Richmond, Rhode Island. 37-year-old Robert Peabody dies.

July 27 – Vietnam War: The U.S. sends 5,000 more military advisers to South Vietnam, bringing the total number of United States forces in Vietnam to 21,000.

July 31 – Ranger program: Ranger 7 sends back the first close-up photographs of the moon (images are 1,000 times clearer than anything ever seen from Earth-bound telescopes).

August 1 – The Final Looney Tune is released before the Warner Bros. Cartoon Division is shut down by Jack Warner.
– Emancipation Day in Barbados, Bermuda, Guyana, St. Vincent and the Grenadines, Trinidad and Tobago, Turks and Caicos Islands, and Jamaica—celebration of the end of slavery in these former and continuing British colonies in the Caribbean.

August 4 – American civil rights movement: The bodies of murdered civil rights workers Michael Schwerner, Andrew Goodman, and James Chaney are found.
– Vietnam War: United States destroyers USS Maddox and USS C. Turner Joy are attacked in the Gulf of Tonkin. Air support from the carrier USS Ticonderoga sinks one gunboat, while the other two leave the battle.

August 5 – Vietnam War: Operation Pierce Arrow – Aircraft from carriers USS Ticonderoga and USS

Constellation bomb North Vietnam in retaliation for strikes against U.S. destroyers in the Gulf of Tonkin.

August 7 – Vietnam War: The United States Congress passes the Gulf of Tonkin Resolution, giving U.S. President Lyndon B. Johnson broad war powers to deal with North Vietnamese attacks on U.S. forces.

August 8 – A Rolling Stones gig gets out of control. Riot police end the gig after about 15 minutes, upon which spectators start to fight the riot police.

August 16 – Vietnam War: In a coup, General Nguyen Khanh replaces Duong Van Minh as South Vietnam's chief of state and establishes a new constitution, drafted partly by the U.S. Embassy.

August 17 – Margaret Harshaw, Metropolitan Opera soprano, sings the role of Turandot in Puccini's opera *Turandot* at the New York World's Fair.

August 20 – International Telecommunications Satellite Consortium.

August 22 – Fannie Lou Hamer, civil rights activist and Vice Chair of the Mississippi Freedom Democratic Party addresses the Credentials Committee of the Democratic National Convention, challenging the all-white Mississippi delegation.

August 24-27 – The Democratic National Convention in Atlantic City nominates incumbent President Lyndon B. Johnson for a full term, and U.S. Senator Hubert Humphrey of Minnesota as his running mate.

August 27 – Walt Disney's *Mary Poppins* has its world premiere in Los Angeles. It will go on to become Disney's biggest moneymaker and winner of five Academy Awards, including a Best Actress award for Julie Andrews, who accepted the part after she was passed over by Jack L. Warner for the leading role of Eliza Dolittle in the film version of *My Fair Lady*. *Mary Poppins* is the first Disney film to be nominated for Best Picture.

August 28-30 – Philadelphia 1964 race riot: Tensions between African American residents and police lead to 341 injuries and 774 arrests.

Orange County, California
El Toro USMC Station 1964

Orange County, California was known for the many, many orange groves located throughout the cities within the County of Orange, California.

Orange County, California was located south of Los Angeles County, north of San Diego County, northeast of San Bernardino County, and southeast of Riverside County, California.

Colonel Jackson, his wife, Joyce, and Yvette, his adopted daughter, arrived at El Toro USMC Station in

Orange County, California on July 1, 1964. They were assigned temporary living quarters until their household goods arrived and their permanent military housing would be available for move-in. He was the new Commanding Officer of the 99th Combat Helicopter Squadron (99th Combat Helicopter unit was responsible for Southeast Asia war missions during Vietnam). Yvette had never lived on a military base before—she had merely visited various military installations during important occasions, events, and ceremonies.

Since their arrival on July 1, 1964, there had been tremendous military ceremonies and preparations for the 4th of July. Colonel Jackson, Joyce, and Yvette were to attend the Change of Command Ceremony, also scheduled during the 4th of July festivities. Yvette was excited about preparing herself once again to wear her Girl Scout uniform for the Change of Command Ceremony with her parents. The 4th of July was a spectacular display of fireworks, parades, and ceremonies. Ten-year-old Yvette was honored to be part of El Toro Marine Base's historical event on July 4, 1964, a day of great value to a little Girl Scout who would one day become a part of history in the making herself...

Colonel Jackson and his newly-adopted ten-year-old daughter, Yvette, made an awesome impression on all the high-ranking military dignitaries; the handsome new Colonel just beamed with pride at Yvette's poise, grace, her Girl Scout Uniform, and her abilities to discuss all that she saw and learned about U.S. American History from her site-seeing tours in Philadelphia and Washington, D.C. with all the high-ranking military dignitaries. She had no difficulties finding herself any new Girl Scout Troops to socialize with during her stay at El Toro Marine Corp Base...

Yvette spent the entire summer touring the coast of Orange County beaches and most of what Southern California had to offer for a summer jammed back of exciting fun in the California sun with her father, Colonel Jackson, her mother, Joyce, and new-found friends from many Girl Scout organizations and groups.

There was Disneyland/Mickey Mouse Club House, Knott's Berry Farm, Magic Mountain, concerts, plays, Hollywood, Universal Studios, TV Game Shows, Griffin Park Conservatory, Irvine Park, Rodeos, Irvine Ranch, lots of beach parties and bar-ques, rock climbing, hiking, biking, and so much more. Even though the summer was about to come to an end, Yvette's popularity was ongoing.

AN ANGEL STANDING BY

Let's give thanks to our heavenly Father for our angel standing by, 'cause it's so wonderful to have someone who rushes to dry each tear we cry... Just a precious guardian angel designed especially to be right by our side, uplifting us when we're low and lonely and comforting us with arms outstretched so wide... Our angel realizes that we're human and protects us when we're weak and often in need... That's why it's so nice to have an angel doing many kindly deeds... Delivering messages of love in a tender, heartfelt way, angels are special and glorious, brightening our day. It's exciting to feel the presence of the angel that God has sent, filling our hearts with hope and happiness as to us they patiently attend...

Walk on in peace and never doubt that Holy Angels do exist... Unnoticed they may come and go—Earth-weary wanderers to assist...

"The Angel of the Son, whose flaming wheels began to run when God's almighty breath said to the Darkness of Light, 'Let there be light!' And there was light... Bringing the gift of Faith."

GODLY GOALS

G – Grab on to His plan

O – Offer to help others...offer kindness

A – Acknowledge Him, honor His plan

L – Leap for joy; joy of the Lord is our strength

S – Service of grateful giving of our time/resources

Kindness is a virtue given by the Lord—it pays dividends in happiness, and joy is its reward. Proverbs 11:18, the wicked man earns deceptive wages, but he who sows righteousness reaps a sure reward...Today add kindness to someone else's life and your own happiness will be multiplied.

- Proverbs 3:5-9, 28:7

Chapter 3

Fall 1964

September 4 – The Forth Road Bridge opens over the Firth of Forth.

September 10 – African Development Bank (AFDB) founded.

September 14 – The third period of the Second Vatican Council opens.

September 16 – *Shindig!* premieres on ABC, featuring the top musical acts of the sixties.

September 17 – *Goldfinger* opens in the UK.
– *Bewitched*, starring Elizabeth Montgomery, premieres on ABC.

September 18 – In Athens, King Constantine II of Greece marries Princess Anne-Marie of Denmark, who becomes Europe's youngest queen at age eighteen years, nineteen days.

– *Johnny Quest* first airs on ABC; featured voices include Mike Road, Tim Mathieson, Don Messick, John Stephenson, and Danny Bravo.

– The North American XB-70 Valkyrie makes its first flight at Palmdale, California.

September 24 – The Warren Commission Report, the first official investigation of the assassination of United States President John F. Kennedy, is published.

October – Dr. Robert Moog demonstrates the prototype Moog synthesizer.

October 1 – Three thousand student activists at the University of California, Berkeley surround and block a police car from taking a CORE volunteer arrested for not showing his ID when he violated a ban on outdoor activist card tables. This protest eventually explodes into the Berkeley Free Speech Movement.

– The Shinkansen high-speed rail system is inaugurated in Japan for the first sector between Tokyo and Osaka.

October 2 – The Kinks release their first album, *The Kinks*.

October 5 – Twenty-three men and thirty-one women escape to West Berlin through a narrow tunnel under the Berlin Wall.

October 10-24 – The 1964 Summer Olympics are held in Tokyo.

October 12 – The Soviet Union launches Voskhod 1 into Earth orbit as the first spacecraft with a multi-person crew and the first flight without space suits. The flight is cut short and lands again on October 13 after 16 orbits.

October 14 – American civil rights movement leader Dr. Martin Luther King, Jr. becomes the youngest recipient of the Nobel Peace Prize, which was awarded to him for leading non-violent resistance to end racial prejudice in the United States.

October 14-15 – Nikita Khrushchev is deposed as leader of the Soviet Union; Leonid Brezhnev and Alexei Kosygin assume power.

October 15 – The Labour Party wins the parliamentary elections in the United Kingdom, ending 13 years of Conservative Party rule. The new prime minister is Harold Wilson.[4]
– Craig Breedlove's jet-powered car, Spirit of America, goes out of control in Bonneville Salt Flats in Utah and makes skid marks 9.6 km long.
– The St. Louis Cardinals defeat the visiting New York Yankees 7–5 to win the World Series in 7 games (4–3), ending a long run of 29 World Series appearances in 44 seasons for the Bronx Bombers (also known as the Yankee Dynasty).

October 16 – Harold Wilson becomes British Prime Minister after leading the Labour Party to a narrow election win over the Tory government of Sir Alec Douglas-Home, which had been in power for 13 years and had four different leaders during that time.

– The People's Republic of China explodes an atomic bomb in Sinkiang.

October 18 – The NY World's Fair closes for the year (it reopens April 21, 1965).

October 21 – The film version of the hit Broadway stage musical *My Fair Lady* premieres in New York City. The movie stars Audrey Hepburn in the role of Eliza Doolittle and Rex Harrison repeating his stage performance as Professor Henry Higgins, and which will win him his only Academy Award for Best Actor. The film will win seven other Academy Awards, including Best Picture, but Audrey Hepburn will not be nominated. Critics interpret this as a rebuke to Jack L. Warner for choosing Ms. Hepburn over Julie Andrews.

October 22 – Canada: A Federal Multi-Party Parliamentary Committee selects a design to become the new official Flag of Canada.

– A 5.3 kiloton nuclear device is detonated at the Tatum Salt Dome, 21 miles (34 km) from Hattiesburg, Mississippi as part of the Vela Uniform program; this test is the Salmon Phase of the Atomic Energy Commission's Project Dribble.

October 27 – In the Democratic Republic of the Congo, rebel leader Christopher Gbenye takes 60 Americans and 800 Belgians hostage.

October 29 – A collection of irreplaceable gemstones, including the 565-carat (113 g) Star of India, is stolen from the American Museum of Natural History in New York City.

October 31 – Campaigning at Madison Square Garden, New York, U.S. President Lyndon Johnson pledges the creation of the Great Society.

*

Yvette was enrolled in school on El Toro US Marine Base in the fall of 1964. This was far different from the New England areas of Washington, D.C., Baltimore, and the City of Brotherly Love that Yvette had become accustomed to—the food, the people, and even the weather was very different in Orange County, California. It was more of a beach party lifestyle all year round. The air of excitement and culture was full of Beach Boy songs, Annette Funicello, Beach Party movies, Stevie Wonder, Jazz on the Beach, Gospel Nights at Disneyland, Praise Nights at Magic Mountain, POP (Pacific Ocean Park), and Student Campus Crusades for Christ events over all high school and college campuses throughout the entire Orange County beach scene culture.

Yvette's school was buzzing with various sports—field hockey, square dancing, tennis, volleyball, and swimming activities for the females. However, the male students had football, basketball, tennis, swimming, and track and field. Yvette was very interested in track and field but there was nothing for the female students in the area of track and field events.

Yvette informed her father, Colonel Jackson, that she was very interested in track and field but her particular school did not have a female team. However, other schools throughout Orange County did, in fact, have their very own female track and field teams...so Colonel Jackson contacted the Orange County School District Athletic Department about his daughter being very interested in track and field and explained that there were no female track and field events within the athletic department at the school she was attending on El Toro USMC Base.

Within a few weeks, it was arranged for Yvette to have a private track and field coach and she was given permission to train with the school's male track and field team. She was even allowed to travel with the male team members to compete as the school's female track and field team representative. Yvette competed in every event except for the relay events. Not only did she compete, she actually excelled in each and every event, taking first place in all that she was allowed to compete in. Yvette soon was making front-page news throughout the sports world in Orange County, California.

Colonel Jackson and Yvette's Track and Field Coach soon organized an Athletic Sports Committee at the Orange County School District Headquarters to assess female sports and athletics within all school levels in the county, soon giving birth to an organization called GAA—Girl's Athletic Association of Orange County. Yvette was soon competing not only in Orange County but throughout the entire State of California. GAA even organized training camps, later giving birth to Title IX of the Education Amendments of 1972, a federal law prohibiting gender discrimination in athletic programs and institutions, thus formulating the Women's Sports Foundation under Title IX in 1972. Yvette and Colonel Jackson were truly a part of history in the making in U.S. American Female Sports and Athletics...

Winter 1964

November 1 – Mortar fire from North Vietnamese forces rains on the Bien Hoa Air Base, killing four U.S. servicemen, wounding 72, and destroying five B-57 jet bombers and other planes.

November 3 – United States presidential election, 1964: Incumbent President Lyndon B. Johnson defeats Republican challenger Barry Goldwater with over 60 percent of the popular vote.

November 5 – Mariner program: Mariner 3, a U.S. space probe intended for Mars, is launched from Cape Kennedy but fails.

November 13 – Bob Pettit (St. Louis Hawks) becomes the first NBA player to score 20,000 points.

November 19 – The United States Department of Defense announces the closing of 95 military bases and facilities, including the Brooklyn Navy Yard, the Brooklyn Army Terminal, and Fort Jay, New York.

November 21 – Second Vatican Council: The third period of the Catholic Church's ecumenical council closes.
– The Verrazano Narrows Bridge opens to traffic (the world's longest suspension bridge at this time).

November 24 – Belgian paratroopers and mercenaries capture Stanleyville, but a number of hostages die in the fighting, among them Evangelical Covenant Church missionary Dr. Paul Carlson.

November 28 – Mariner program: NASA launches the Mariner 4 space probe from Cape Kennedy toward Mars to take television pictures of the planet in July 1965.
– Vietnam War: United States National Security Council members, including Robert McNamara, Dean Rusk, and Maxwell Taylor, agree to recommend a plan for a 2-stage escalation of bombing in North Vietnam to President Lyndon B. Johnson.
– France performs underground nuclear test at Ecker in Algeria.

December 1 – Gustavo Díaz Ordaz takes office as President of Mexico.
– Vietnam War: U.S. President Lyndon B. Johnson and his top-ranking advisers meet to discuss plans to bomb North Vietnam (after some debate, they agree on a 2-phase

bombing plan).

December 3 – Berkeley Free Speech Movement: Police arrest about 800 students at the University of California, Berkeley, following their takeover of and massive sit-in at the Sproul Hall administration building. The sit-in most directly protested the U.C. Regents' decision to punish student activists for what many thought had been justified civil disobedience earlier in the conflict.

December 6 – The one-hour stop-motion animated special *Rudolph the Red-Nosed Reindeer*, based on the popular Christmas song, premieres on NBC. It becomes a beloved Christmas tradition, still being shown on television more than 40 years later.

December 10 – Dr. Martin Luther King, Jr. awarded Nobel Peace Prize in Oslo, Norway.

December 11 – Che Guevara addresses the U.N. General Assembly.

December 14 – Heart of Atlanta Motel v. United States (379 US 241 1964): The U.S. Supreme Court rules that, in accordance with the Civil Rights Act of 1964, establishments providing public accommodations must refrain from racial discrimination.

December 15 – The *Washington Post* publishes an article about James Hampton, who had built a glittering religious throne out of recycled materials.

December 18 – In the wake of deadly riots in January over control of the Panama Canal, the U.S. offers to negotiate a new canal treaty.

– The deadly Christmas flood of 1964 begins; it becomes one of the most destructive weather events to affect Oregon in the 20th century.

December 21 – The James Bond film *Goldfinger* begins its run in U.S. theaters. It becomes one of the most successful and popular Bond films ever made.

– The General Dynamics F-111 Aardvark makes its first flight.

– The Lockheed SR-71 Blackbird makes its first flight at Palmdale, California.

December 23 – Wonderful Radio London commences transmissions with American top 40 formats broadcasting from a ship anchored off the south coast of England.

December 26 – Lesley Ann Downey, 10, is abducted by Ian Brady and Myra Hindley in Manchester, England.

December 27 – The Cleveland Browns defeat the Baltimore Colts in the National Football League Championship Game.

December 30 – United Nations Conference on Trade and Development (UNCTAD) established as a permanent organ of the UN General Assembly.

*

Yvette continued her track and field training off-season in the early morning or early evenings, running the entire inner boundary perimeter of El Toro USMC Base, which is measured as a total of 32 square miles in circumference. During her training sessions, Yvette would meet several migrant agriculture workers and their children working the agriculture farming areas of El Toro USMC Base. The children of the workers began asking Yvette questions about what she was doing and what she was training for. She simply told them that she was a future Olympic Athletic in training. They asked Yvette if they could learn to train with her. "Why, sure," she said. Little did Yvette know that those same children grew up to change the course of history in Southern California...they entered the Los Angeles Marathon and won, which opened the door of opportunity for the future of other children of field agriculture farm workers. Yvette would soon meet Uncle CC, aka César Chavez, who was an American labor leader and civil rights activist who founded the National Farm Workers Association in 1962.

VIETNAM WAR...

The Vietnam War (Vietnamese: Chin tranh Vit Nam, in Vietnam known as the American War, Vietnamese: Chin tranh M, Kháng chin chng M), also known as the Second Indochina War, was a Cold War-era military conflict that occurred in Vietnam, Laos, and Cambodia from November 1, 1955 to the fall of Saigon on April 30, 1975. This war followed the First Indochina War and was fought between

North Vietnam—supported by China and other communist allies—and the government of South Vietnam—supported by the United States and other anti-communist countries. The Viet Cong (also known as the National Liberation Front, or NLF), a lightly armed South Vietnamese communist common front directed by the North, largely fought a guerrilla war against anti-communist forces in the region. The Vietnam People's Army (North Vietnamese Army) engaged in a more conventional war, at times committing large units into battle. U.S. and South Vietnamese forces relied on air superiority and overwhelming firepower to conduct search and destroy operations involving ground forces, artillery, and airstrikes.

The U.S. government viewed American involvement in the war as a way to prevent a communist takeover of South Vietnam. This was part of their wider strategy of containment, which aimed to stop the spread of communism. The North Vietnamese government and the Viet Cong were fighting to reunify Vietnam under communist rule. They viewed the conflict as a colonial war, fought initially against France, then against America as France was backed by the U.S., and later against South Vietnam, which it regarded as a U.S. puppet state. Beginning in 1950, American military advisers arrived in what was then French Indochina. U.S. involvement escalated in the early 1960s, with troop levels tripling in 1961 and again in 1962. U.S. combat units were deployed beginning in 1965. Operations crossed international borders, with Laos and Cambodia heavily bombed. American involvement in the war peaked in 1968, at the time of the Tet Offensive. After this, U.S. ground forces were gradually withdrawn as part of a policy known as Vietnamization, which aimed to end American involvement in the war. Despite the Paris Peace Accords, which were signed by all parties in January 1973, the fighting continued.

U.S. military involvement ended on August 15, 1973 as a result of the Case–Church

Amendment passed by the U.S. Congress. The capture of Saigon by the Vietnam People's Army in April 1975 marked the end of the war, and North and South Vietnam were reunified the following year. The war exacted a huge human cost in terms of fatalities. Estimates of the number of Vietnamese service members and civilians killed vary from 800,000 to 3.1 million. Some 200,000-300,000 Cambodians, 20,000-200,000 Laotians, and 58,220 U.S. service members also died in the conflict.

TIMELINE OF THE YEAR 1964 (a leap year)

It wasn't before long that Colonel Jackson and his El Toro USMC Base helicopter units were all well on their way to Southeast Asia. To keep from missing her father, Yvette began to train even harder than ever before in various cross-training sports and athletic activities such as field hockey, tennis, volleyball, and she even became the school mascot. One day while she was running the entire inner boundary perimeter of El Toro USMC Base, Yvette heard a voice calling to her, "Hey Meeha," the voice said, "come here! The children have been telling me about you, they are calling you! They are calling you 'Crazy L'eggs Jackson!'" Yvette began laughing. "Crazy L'eggs," she said, then she began laughing again. The strange man's face shone in the morning sun as he laughed along with Yvette. His skin was a golden brown and a little worn from much sun exposure, his chest and shoulders broad and strong, much like many of the USMC men stationed at El Toro Marine base. "Let me introduce myself, I am César Chavez, but please just call me Uncle CC. I used to be in the U.S. Navy and I was once stationed here at El Toro USMC Base but now I am the founding President of the National Farm Workers Associations! Is your father stationed here at El Toro?" he asked. Yvette told Uncle CC that her father and his helicopter division were on their way to Southeast Asia. César Chavez could see the sadness in Yvette's eyes. "Well I would love to meet your mother, is she home?" he asked. "Well, I think so," she said. He asked, "What is your home telephone number? I'll give her a call right now! Hey Meeha," he said, "I got your address from your mother and I told her that I will treat the both of you to some real Mexican Soul Food! Have you ever had Authentic Mexican food before?" he asked her. Yvette asked him, "Is Mexican Style foods anything like Cuban style cuisine?" He told her there were some similarities but many of the spices were a little different. From that day forth, whenever Uncle CC was in the Orange County area, he would come and pick Yvette up in his pick-up truck and take her to the various Farm Worker Camps located throughout the Orange County areas, which was known for an abundance of citrus fruit crops and other various agriculture crops grown throughout the region, such as lettuce, tomatoes, onions, strawberries, grapes, soy beans, avocados, etc. Yvette would run with the migrant workers' children and grandchildren throughout the fields and teach them proper racing form, body posture form, and proper alignment techniques. Yvette would then organize races among the boys and girls and set up relay teams at each individual agriculture farming agriculture camp—there were well over 177 migrant camps throughout the Orange County area that Uncle CC and Yvette traveled to within 32 weeks between 1964 and1965.

César Chavez saw the sadness in Yvette's eyes soon turn to a purposeful meaning for all the migrant children and their families at the farming camps. Yvette and Uncle CC were actually setting up what is referred to today as "YOUTH SUMMER SPORTS CAMPS!" Yvette organized sports training sessions and even English classes along with what she called her "Olympic athletes in training" sessions.

The Value of Time Is The Value of Life...

How valuable is your time today?
How do you value each day?
How do you value each moment?
How do you value each minute?
How do you value each hour?

God Saves The Humble Person...

Though the LORD is on high,
he looks upon the lowly,
but the proud he knows from afar.

Psalm 138:6 NIV

He shall save the humble person.

Job 22:29 KJV

But he gives more grace; therefore it says, "God opposes the proud, but gives grace to the humble." Submit yourselves therefore to God. Resist the devil and he will flee from you.

James 4:6,7 RSV

O LORD, You have heard the desire of the humble;
You will strengthen their heart,
You will incline Your ear to vindicate
the orphan and the oppressed,
So that man who is of the earth
will no longer cause terror.

Psalm 10:17, 18 NASB

Thanks be unto God for His wonderful gift:
Jesus Christ, the only begotten Son of God
is the object of our faith; the only faith
that saves is faith in Him.

A Time for Everything...

To everything there is a season,
and a time to every purpose under the heaven:

A time to be born, and a time to die;
a time to plant, and a time to pluck up that which is
     planted;

A time to kill, and a time to heal;
a time to break down, and a time to build up;
A time to weep, and a time to laugh;
a time to mourn, and a time to dance;

A time to cast away stones,
and a time to gather stones together;
a time to embrace, and
a time to refrain from embracing;

A time to get, and a time to lose;
a time to keep, and a time to cast away;

A time to rend, and a time to sew;
a time to keep silence, and a time to speak;

A time to love, and a time to hate;
a time of war, and a time of peace.

Ecclesiastes 3:1-8 KJV

Chapter 4

ALLELUIA ABUNDANT BLESSINGS!!!

What can I pray for that Christ hasn't done for you already? If I say long life, it's your inheritance in HIM already. If I say favor, it's your portions already. If I say peace, I know you will dwell in the secret place of the most high. And if I say collective fulfillment and abundant blessings, it's already yours in HIM. May this be a time of answered prayers and gracious fulfillment, and may you go from Glory to Glory in HIM!

GOD'S LOVE

Long ago, one silent night, GOD revealed HIS glory bright; HIS own image came to man... For salvation's matchless plan. Jesus, Savior, Shepherd, and King—Lord of all to you we bring... Praises, wonder, thanks, and love; for this gift from GOD above... (Luke 19:10)

The Son of man has come to seek and to save that which was lost...TAKING GOD SERIOUSLY.
GOD occupies first place in everything...
HIS word is the final word in everything...
Worship HIM deep and meaningful...
The value we embrace will transcend cultures and not be based on them.
The integrity of the family is love, trust, and honesty...

Church is our College
Heaven is our University
Jesus is our Principal
The Holy Spirit is our Teacher
Angels are our Classmates
The Bible is our Study Book
Trial & Temptation are our Exams
Winning Souls are our Assignments
Prayer is our attendance
Crown of Life is our Degree
Praise & Worship is our Motto
Enroll today there is room for all...and tuition is free!!

POSITIVE WORD THOUGHTS

F U T U R E =
F – Faith U – Ultimate T – Truth U – Unity R – Refine
E - Excellence

P O W E R =
P – Purpose O - Opportunity W - Wisdom E - Excel R - Respect

T R U = Trusting - Revealing – Understanding
"Difference is that raw & powerful connection from which our personal power is forged."

A B C = Amazing Blessings Campaign = Heaven's Humanity!

A M A Z I N G = A - Able M - Meaning A - Affectively Z - Zest I - Inspire N - Needful G - Gracious

B L E S S I N G S = B - Best L - Loyal E - Enthusiasm S - Spiritual S - Seeds I - Industrial N - Noble G - Grounded S - Sowing

C A M P A I G N = C - Compassion A - Admiration M - Mutual P - Positive A - Affective I - Intelligent G - Graceful N - Nurturing

UC – UNIVERAL CONNECTIVITY

We cannot grasp formless, of the oneness we are seeing, emptiness is the inner nature within the outer form of being... Life is a journey, not a destination continuing, forwarding pathways into stages...into phase...into an incredible journey... As water has been primary to the life of the earth, Universal Connectivity (UC) has been fundamental to the spiritual vitality of the world. UC inspires us to awaken a deeper feeling about life; it touches the hearts of humankind everywhere to bestow upon the universe...

Novices often have little understanding of the multifaceted history and complex evolution of the laws that govern the universe. It continues to flow on its journey to many cultures over the centuries.

UC can be expressed and enhanced through everyday life, in work and play, in art and sports; it transforms the mundane into the sublime, the temporal into the eternal. The human mind becomes one with its inner spirit, refreshed with the waters of UC.

UC's journey around the world presents a history, but as a spiritual odyssey. Gathered together are the entire pathway, stages, and phases of UC. The journey unfolds before you as a spiritual companion traveling across time and space, circling the globe. There is intellectual foundation for understanding UC's passage around the world, which offers us help to gain a clearer foundation of what is so relevant to us all. UC points directly to the spirit that shines like a beacon in the night to show us the Way into these pathways, stages, and phases into a universal journey. Developing and embracing diversity, and yet through it all, the spirit of UC is always present.

Spiritual interaction between to be; is transmitted to help create the enlightenment of practical interaction within oneness, coming from something wonderful with a higher consciousness. Spiritual practice of meditation is the discovery of a long-established advance awakening, a disciplined method of focusing attention and clearing the mind to achieve union with the universe.

The theory is toward true nature and harmony that encompasses everything. The entire thrust of contending a universal, spiritual principle that we are all a part of and yet lies beyond us; seeking to yield to an experience of unity with inspiration and guidance. The source of meaning is the spiritual way of things, united to gain wisdom through the word of "God," sensitivity, and insight. This brings about the union of seeking balance, to include both sides to be unified in the wholeness within a pathway to allow the natural course of events to take place. The order of acquiring knowledge, in becoming one with order of happiness, fulfillment, and true wisdom of humanity is inherently an expression of giving balance to a fuller, tranquil conception of peace within; allowing permeated structured renunciation of a positive view of humanity, and harmony with the universal law of "God" that governs our "Way," joined with the path to truth, to reaching understanding...as the light of dawning into a profound horizon.

The essence to achieve direct to a powerful force emerging fertile developmental flowering influences profound inspiration that touches a reawakening, rekindling to flourishing a deep spiritual understanding of our own true nature; this is the beginning root to an ultimate existence of one's inner nature. This is an emerging demonstration of a logical link equivalent to conception and co-existing with the fulfillment of fullness which is the opposition of emptiness. It is defined by virtue of contrast parts of component parts bolted together in synthesis. As an analogy compounded together through inter-relationship to exist as a unity and being codependent. Existing only through contrast to the other, threads within the tapestry releasing the ascetic achievement to transitory peaceful conceptualized of legitimate comprehensible growth; to a developed management of a devoted functional positive statement to a clear lifestyle management supported by, to, and for passages giving us pathway stages and phases into a journey...WITH COLORS OF THE RAINBOW & BEYOND.

The rainbow is not located at a specific distance, but from a certain angle. Thus, a rainbow is not an object, and cannot be physically approached. Indeed, it is impossible for an observer to see a rainbow from any angle other than the customary one of 42 degrees from the directional opposite. Even if an observer sees another observer who seems "under" or "at the end of" a rainbow, the second observer will see a different rainbow—further off—at the same angle as seen by the first observer. A rainbow spans a continuous spectrum of colors. Any distinct bands perceived are an artifact of human color vision, and no banding of any type is seen in a black-and-white photo of a rainbow, only a smooth gradation of intensity to a maximum, then fading towards the other side. For colors seen by the human eye, the most commonly cited and remembered sequence is seven-fold red, orange, yellow, green, blue, and indigo/violet.

The colors of the rainbow are fresh, vibrant, cheerful, and amazingly deep. Seeing a rainbow can easily improve the mood of all people, making them feel better and happier. The seven colors of the rainbow emanate; the primary colors are red, yellow, and blue. From these colors emanate orange, green, indigo, and violet.

RAINBOW COLORS AND THEIR MEANING

1. Blue
Blue is one of the most powerful colors of the rainbow. This is the color of distance, oceans, and skies, but also the color of the heavens. Blue has always been considered a color of energy, expanding perceptions to the unknown. Blue is also thought to be the color of divinity. This color is able to bring peace and understanding, calm and relaxation. The color also enhances communication and offers a feeling of peace and happiness. It expresses spirituality.

2. Yellow
Yellow is the color of the sun. It expresses energy and life. This color brings clarity of thought, orderliness, and memory improvement, but it is also able to alleviate confusion and improve decision-making skills. This is the color of wisdom.

3. Red
Red has always been considered the color of passion. This is the color of activity, too. Red sustains physical body movement and brings energy and enthusiasm, but also passion and security. Red stands for vitality.

4. Orange
Orange combines two colors: red and yellow—so it includes both energy and wisdom. Orange is considered to be a color of dynamic energy, bringing creativity, playfulness, relief from boredom, and equilibrium.

5. Green

Green has always been the color of life. The human eye is able to recognize more variations of green than any other color. This color expresses harmony, health, balance, and abundance, but also sympathy and growth.

6. Indigo

Indigo is believed to amplify energy in a more profound way than blue. It expresses wisdom, sudden awareness, and abilities.

7. Violet

Violet is considered to be the ray of spiritual mastery. Violet is formed by a combination of red and blue. It brings energy and is associated with spiritual attainment and healing.

****

****

Rainbows are considered to be a unique, impressive spectacle of nature...

1. Every time we see a rainbow, it's after the rain. It means that the sun is always behind you and the rain in front of you when a rainbow appears. Thus, the center of the rainbow's arc is directly opposite the sun.

2. Many believe that the colors of the rainbow are only red, orange, yellow, green, blue, and indigo, but a rainbow is formed from numerous colors, even from those we can't see.

3. People can see the colors of a rainbow due to the light of various colors that are refracted when going from one medium, such as air, into another—in our case, the

raindrops formed from water.

4. Every one of us sees our own "personal" rainbow. When you look at a rainbow, for example, you see the lights reflected off certain raindrops, while the person next to you, looking at the same rainbow, may see the light reflecting from a different angle, so it's different. It means that every person sees rainbow colors according to light and how their eyes perceive it.

5. The end of a rainbow can never be reached. When you move, the rainbow that you see with your eyes moves as well as the raindrops found in various spots in the atmosphere. In a few words, the rainbow will move always while you are moving, at the same rate. People are happier when seeing a rainbow.

****

****

SPIRITUAL COLORS OF OUR RAINBOW & BEYOND... ATTITUDE, PERSPECTIVE, PASSION & POWER

Chapter 5

A T T I T U D E: The longer you live, the more you will realize the impact of attitude on life... Attitude is more important than facts. It is more important than appearance, gifts, or skills. It will make or break a company, a church, a home, and/or a marriage. The remarkable thing is that we have a choice every day regarding the attitude we will embrace for that day. We cannot change our past...we cannot change the fact that people will act in a certain way. We cannot change the inevitable. Life is 10% what happens to us and 90% how we react to it...and so, "YOU" are in charge of your attitude, which determines your attitude in life...ATTITUDE IS YOU reaching your altitude potential.

P E R S P E C T I V E: Extending to a distance; a vista. The manner in which objects appear in respect to their relative position in one's mental view, fact and/or ideas, and their interrelationships. The ability to see all the relevant data in meaningful relationships.

PERSPECTIVE IS
SPIRITUAL
ABILITIES...

PASSION: A compelling, strong, amorous feeling; love, desire, fondness, enthusiasm for something. The object or an outburst of passion... PASSION IS WITHIN.

POWER: An ability to do or the act of doing or accomplishing something; the capability marked by the ability to or act. The possession of command, authority to influence. Ascendancy position of great forceful spiritual strength... *SPIRITUAL COLORS OF OUR RAINBOW & BEYOND********

POISE: A state of balance or equilibrium, as from equality or equal distribution; a dignified, self-confident manner, bearing, or composure of steadiness; stability of the way of being poised, held, or carried. The state of positioning to adjust or carry in equilibrium balance evenly... POWER OF POISE.

Thank you Uncle CC—aka César E. Chávez:

César E. Chávez: American labor leader and civil rights activist who founded the National Farm Workers Association; a great Mexican American; best-known Latino American civil rights activist.
****
****
Understanding purposeful determination through the measure of his foundation is the cornerstone...

They Will Soar On Wings Like Eagles. (Isaiah 40:31)

GOD'S PROMISE TO US IS STRENGTH

The Lord is my light and my salvation; whom shall I fear? (Psalm 27:1)

The Lord is the strength of my life; of who shall I be afraid? I will strengthen thee; yea, and I will help thee; yea, I will uphold thee with the right hand of my righteousness. (Isaiah 41:10)

HONOR, PRAISE & THANKS!!!

23 Psalm – For the Christian in Business and Work Place:
The Lord is my real boss, and I shall not want.
He gives me peace when chaos is all around me.
He gently reminds me to pray before I speak and to do all things without complaining.

He reminds me that He is my Source and not my job.

He restores my sanity every day and guides my decisions that I might honor Him in everything I do.

Even though I face absurd amounts of unrealistic deadlines, budget cutbacks, and an aging body that doesn't cooperate every day, I will not stop—for He is with me! His presence, His peace, and His power will see me through.

He raises me up even when others do not.

He claims me as His own, even when things seem dark.

His faithfulness and love are always better!

When it's all said and done, I'll be working for Him a whole lot longer and for that, I bless His name...

THE GOVERNMENT OF GOD

1. Minister of finance
Haggai 2:8 – Silver & gold are mine.
2. Minster of Education
Hosea 4:6 – My people perish because of lack of knowledge.
3. Minister of Roads
John 14:6 – I am the way, the truth & the life. No one comes to my Father except through me.
4. Minister of Tourism
Mark 16:15 – Go into all corners of the world & preach good news to every creature.
5. Minister of Labor
Matt 9:37 – Harvest is abundant but workers are few.
6. Minister of Sports
1 Corinthians 9:24, 27 – Be like an athlete; run so that you will be the first.
7. Minister of Transportation
Matthew 11:28 – Come to me, all who are tired from carrying heavy loads, and I will give you rest.
8. Minister of Health
Isaiah 53:5 – He took our infirmities; we are healed.
9. Minister of Internal Security
Isaiah 54:17 – No weapon formed against me shall prosper.
10. Minister of Agriculture
John 15:1 – I am the true vine & my Father is the gardener. He cuts off every branch in me that bears no fruits.
11. Minister of Faith
(Hebrews 11:1; Hebrews 6:17; Ephesians 2:8-9)

Divine Diagnosis
The Sovereignty of God!

Chapter 6

ELEVATED E-BOOK CLUB
DESIGNED FOR COMMUNITY, SMALL GROUP STUDY &
COMMUNITY LEADERSHIP GROWTH!

E L E V A T E D:
Empowering
Lifted
Enhancing
Validation
Accountability
Testament
Educate
Duty

PROVERBS 8
"GOD's" WISDOM

5 – E L E V A T E D

E-BOOK CLUB, BOOKS BY RHONDA DULA

1. *Transformed by HIS Presence: God's Transformation*
ASIN: B077BKR3HY
Description: Breaking Through A Blessed Life... Experiencing Spiritual Breakthrough(s)!

2. *Walking A Godly Life: A Transformation*
ASIN: B076RLKC85
Description: A Daily Walk with God – Church is my College, Heaven is my University, Jesus is my Principal, the Holy Spirit is my Teacher, Angels are my Classmates—Enroll today, there is room for all and tuition is free...

3. *The Essence of Life: The Super Puzzle Pieces*
ASIN: B07779TTS4
Description: Achieving dreams means building values for others in turn brings happiness... Love is the reward in life for making values and building values... "Once A Upon A Midnight Clear."

4. *The Journey: AG – Amazing Grace (Leadership Development Series #1)*
ASIN: B076RMF16K
Description: "Journey" to living the truth...it all starts now! It all starts with you! This is your adventure in a better, brighter future and it begins with developing leadership potential within you...

5. *Once Upon A Midnight Clear: God's Love For Us*
ASIN: B077GY7BY6

Description: (Words of Wisdom) – There comes a time in your life when you finally get it; when in the midst of the fears and insanity in this world, you stop dead in your tracks and, somewhere, the voice inside you cries out, "ENOUGH, IS ENOUGH, our "GOD's" love is bigger and better than anything that this world is trying to offer!!!" In the midnight hour it becomes very, very clear that "GOD's" mercy, grace, and goodness is enough!!!

FUTURE – Amazon Kindle E-books

Rhonda Dula's Pending Projects:
6 Future Elevated E-Club Books:

The Calling

He Wore a Crown

Uncle CC & Me – The Girl Scout Effect Part II (children's e-book, in Spanish)

Thanks, Honor & Praise

Black Orange

WIN – Women's International Network

E L E V A T E D: Empowering, Lifted, Enhancing, Validation, Accountability, Testament, Educate, and Duty

VISION STATEMENT:
L.I.F.E.: L = LEARNING I = INSPIRATION F = FOUNDATION E = ENRICHMENT

LEARNING ENRICHMENT IS NOT A DESTINATION...IT IS A HIGHER METHOD OF LIFE.

THE 5 WS: WHO/WHAT/WHEN/WHERE/WHY = HOW TO LOOK FOR CAUSE & AFFECT

AIMS AND MISSION OBJECTIVES: Supporting, developing, creating, identifying, and capturing change impact relevant to progressive life skills. Implement feedback on change execution and developing ideas for improvement and provide input for approach. Work with team(s) to define change structure and identify potential life skill growth.

EDUCATION ESSENTIALS: Well-organized small groups, performing and causing the stated action within aims and mission objectives, formulating teamwork. Spiritual abundance and prosperity even during times of adversity.

TRAINING/SKILLS: Hardworking, achieving goals, discipline, orderly, planning, self-confidence, patience, determination, stamina, courage, faith, hope, strength, and loyalty. Persistent, consistent, being determined even in the face of tragedy will result in victory.

PROFESSIONAL ACCOMPLISHMENTS: Develop leadership skills through the application of new concepts and creative approaches that will help meet the challenges of the present and anticipate the needs of the future. Support innovation and agility within basic ethical foundational structures by providing resourceful information that reaches the core of confidence and vision by harnessing and developing educational application and by use of applied potential.

Leadership Ethics Series – 15 life skills of leadership enrichment ethics series, equipped with instructor/ associates guides; Sole purpose for community leadership development foundation education. 15 L.I.F.E. Skills Ethics Series Foundation as listed:

1. TIME MANAGEMENT
2. PUBLIC SPEAKING
3. PRESENTATION SKILLS
4. ORGANIZATIONAL SKILLS
5. NEGOTIATING SKILLS
6. MANAGER MANAGEMENT
7. LEADERSHIP AND INFLUENCE
8. DELIVERING CONSTRUCTIVE CRITICISM
9. CRITICAL THINKING
10. COMMUNICATION STRATEGIES
11. CONFLICT RESOLUTION
12. COACHING AND MENTORING
13. BUSINESS ETHICS
14. TEAMWORK AND TEAM BUILDING

15. BUSINESS ACUMEN
3 × 5 PHASE CONCEPT

PHASE I
1. Business Acumen
2. Business Ethics
3. Coaching & Mentoring
4. Teamwork & Team Building
5. Leadership & Influence

PHASE II
1. Communication Strategies
2. Critical Thinking
3. Negotiation Skills
4. Delivering Constructive Criticism
5. Conflict Resolution

PHASE III
1. Manager Management
2. Time Management
3. Organizational Skills
4. Public Speaking
5. Presentation Skills

Chapter 7

Characteristics of a Godly Individual Overcoming Adversity

Refinement - Sin - Surrender - Repentance - Attention
John 16:33, Adversity

THE BOOK OF JOB

Chapter 1
Verses 1-5 (Introduction) Spiritually mature with wisdom, measure spiritual uprightness
Verses 6-22 (Testing) Upholding faith maturity

Chapter 2
(Loyalty) Continue to praise him through the adversity

Chapter 3
(Compassion) Inspiration and encouragement through comfort

Chapter 4
(Transformation) Friendship in adversity

Chapter 5
(Correction) Building character

SPIRITUAL RISK MANAGEMENT ENRICHMENT PROCESS

STEP 1 – COLLECT DATA AND INFORMATION
The systematic collection of data used to comprehend the risk universe, gain a historical perspective of the identified risk, and establish a baseline risk.

STEP 2 – ANALYZE AND ASSESS RISK
Use of analytical tools to determine the areas of greatest risk and scope of the problem in those areas.

STEP 3 – PRESCRIBE ACTION
Design a course of action and assign appropriate resources to address the determined risk.

STEP 4 – TRACK AND REPORT
Results are compiled and reported back into the "Risk Management Process" for monitoring of future action.

THE POWER OF THE POSITIVE

A world where everyone receives applause, where we all cheer with hope and breathe with optimism!

Fortunately, there is a magic potion that makes our ordinary lives special and enriched. It is having the insight to see the same thing in a different way—to be positive. When you want to give up, when things are so difficult that you cannot cope, try taking a deep, deep breath...try taking a stroll through a beautiful green forest in your mind. Eventually, breathing, like hope, will enable you to keep going. Before you know it, the growing power of the positive will help you create dreams for the future, and having these dreams will bring you happiness. Try closing your eyes now. When you close your eyes, you can focus on yourself. Say to yourself sincerely, "I give thanks to the heavens, I give thanks to humanity, and I give thanks to mother earth," and then give yourself a big hug. Don't live according to others' standards, waiting to receive applause. Give yourself your own applause—also, don't forget to applaud others no matter what! Become a flower blooming in the desert! Always strive to do your best no matter what! Even if it is something small, your great soul will continue to grow pure. Give praise and give applause. What about the sun that rose again today? Rather than being lazy, the sun rose again to make us warm. Isn't this enough to deserve applause and give thanks?

Expressing gratitude and appreciation shouldn't be difficult. Nor should it be something saved for special occasions. All life is worthy of applause simply because it exists. Why don't we change the tendency in our society to only give applause for exceptional abilities or excellence? Why don't we try creating a world in which everyone can receive applause? Let's give ourselves, our family, our friends, and our colleagues applause. Then, when we feel worn out and tired, at least we won't feel alone because someone will be cheering over our shoulder. Finding small miracles in everyday life and believing in the soul's positivity and the happiness of wisdom.

Our face is a smile box. Not a box with a smiley face on it, but a box containing something that makes others smile too! There are two good ways to make your face bright. These are none other than positive thinking and smiling. This is nothing other than a miracle of life; bringing hope will be able to create miracles in everyday life. Just act positive! If you act positive, you will become positive. Breathe hope! Hope comes in, desperation goes out. If you breathe hope, you don't need to call for it desperately. If you breathe hope, you don't need to feel afraid. Breathe hope!

They Will Soar On Wings Like Eagles. (Isaiah 40:31)

God's Promise To Us Is...Strength

The Lord is my light and my salvation; whom shall I fear? (Psalm 27:1)

The Lord is the strength of my life; of who shall I be afraid? I will strengthen thee; yea, I will help thee; yea, I will uphold thee with the right hand of my righteousness. (Isaiah 41:10)

"TEACH US TO NUMBER OUR DAYS"
TIME – MAKE THE MOST OF IT!

Our days are identical to suitcases, but some people pack more into theirs than others. That's because they know what to pack. Everybody gets twenty-four hours, but not everybody gets the same return on their twenty-four hours. The truth is, you don't manage your time—you manage your life. Time cannot be controlled; it marches on no matter what you do. Nobody—no matter how shrewd—can save minutes. With all his wealth, Warren Buffett can't buy additional hours for his day. People talk about trying to "find time," but they need to quit looking; there isn't any extra lying around. Twenty-four hours is the best any of us is going to get. Wise people understand that time is their most precious commodity. As a result, they know where their time goes. They continually analyze how they are using their time and ask themselves, "Am I getting the best use out of my time?"
In his book, "What To Do Between Birth and Death: The Art of Growing UP," *Charles Spezzano writes: "You don't really pay for things with money, you pay for them with time. We say 'In five years, I'll have enough money put away for that vacation house we want. Then I'll slow down.' That means the house will cost you five years—one-twelfth of your adult life. Translate the dollar value of the house, car, or anything else into time, and then see if it's still worth it."*

"ABOUT COMMITMENTS"

When you measure your life by the yardstick, you have a better chance of living by the right commitments. There are three types of commitments:

(1) Dramatic Commitments. Like getting married or buying a home. Unfortunately, we don't consider the hidden costs. When we buy a house we think only of the additional square footage, not the extra hour each day commuting to work or the time taken away from our family.

(2) Routine Commitments.

(3) Unspoken Commitments. These are the commitments we make to ourselves but often fail to keep. In life, the dramatic commitments receive most of our attention, but the routine ones end up controlling us. Because there are so many of them and because they come on a daily basis and individually look so small, we don't sense the gap growing between what we say matters most to us and what we're actually doing with our lives... So let's simplify it: "Love the Lord and love your neighbor. Amen."

EDUCATIONAL OBJECTIVES

Introduce organizational development skills through the application of new concepts and creative approaches that will help meet the challenges of the present and anticipate the needs of the future of your organization through humor and illustration. Support innovation and agility within your organizational structure by providing resourceful information so that new solutions reach the core of the mission and organization's vision. Harness and develop learning applications within your institution with procedural management tools by using applied technology information systems. With merited abilities to communicate orally and in writing effectively, conducting and maintaining professional educational integrity, with limited personnel of various multicultural diverse backgrounds, while managing multiple assignments, settings deadlines, and overseeing challenging situations while remaining flexible and effective.

WALKING A GODLY LIFE
2 Peter 1:4

Just think...we're here not by chance, but by God's choosing. His hand formed us and made us the person we are.

He compares us to no one else—we are one of a kind. We lack nothing that His grace can't give us.

He has allowed us to be here at this time in history to fulfill His special purpose for this generation.

We are God's servants in God's place at God's perfect time.

He has given us His very great and precious promises, so that through them we may participate in the divine nature.

Do not be anxious about anything, but in everything, by prayer and petition with thanksgiving, present your requests to God. - Phil 4:6

LIFE IN GOD'S GARDEN

While working in my garden, in the warm and flowing sun, I thought of life and how our Lord tends sweetly to each one. We prune and clip and till the soil and watch as flowers grow, their beauty made much richer as each time we deeply sow. So is our life—God prunes and clips then watches for the blooms, watches for the fruit of life, as tenderly He looms. And steadfastness in pruning surely brings the sweetest fruit, like faith and patience, peace and trust, when God becomes our root...

LEADERSHIP DEVELOPMENT INITIATIVE

PROGRAM OBJECTIVE
Introduce professional development skills through the application of new concepts and creative approaches that will help meet the challenges of the present and anticipate the needs of the future. Support innovation and agility within basic ethical foundational structures by providing resourceful information so that new solutions reach the core of the vision by harnessing leadership development educational application(s) and management tools by use of applied classroom instructional guidance.

CORE VALUES
Accountability
Stewardship
Commitment

Respect
Integrity
Service
Loyalty
Growth

Educational partnership and leadership development through community service activities in developing preparations within prospective communities; with the usage of oral communications and in writing, through meetings/group activities (such as Non-Government Organizations (NGOs), all levels of government departments, college/university campuses, festivals, workshops, seminars, media events, film productions, stage productions, school events, churches, businesses, and institutions). Conduct and maintain professional business integrity with various multicultural diverse backgrounds.

7 COMMON ELEMENTS
OF A HEALTHY LEADERSHIP TEAM

What fosters team spirit? What makes a healthy leadership team?

All of us want that. I would even say especially leaders.

Most of us understand that progress towards a vision is more possible if a healthy team is working together.

Also, all of us want to go home at night feeling like we've done our best, were appreciated for our efforts, and are ready to go at it again tomorrow. That's part of serving on a healthy team.

How do we get there?

I've served—and led—many teams throughout my career. Some I would say were healthy, some weren't, and some were "under construction." I take complete ownership of each of those. Team leadership spirit—healthy teams—are greatly shaped by the leadership of the team (and that's a hard word when, as a leader, we know the team isn't as healthy as it should be).

Among the healthy teams on which I've served, there have been some common elements.

Here are seven common elements of a healthy team:

1. Clear strategy.

To feel a part of the team, people need to know where the team is going and what their role is on the team. An understanding of the overall goals and objectives fuels energy. When the big picture objective is understood, each team member is more willing to pull together to accomplish the mission because they know the *why* and can better understand where they fit on the team.

2. Healthy relationships.

For a team to have team spirit, it needs to be filled with team members who actually like each other and enjoy spending time with one another.

3. Celebratory atmosphere.

Laughter builds community. A team needs time just to have fun together. And there needs to be freedom for spontaneous (and planned) celebration. People need to feel appreciated for their work and that their participation is making a positive difference.

4. Joint ownership.

This one is huge, because without it the team won't be completely healthy. Some people are not team players. Period. They checked out years ago and are now just drawing a paycheck—or continuing to hold onto a title. They may be great people, but they aren't building team spirit anymore. They don't want to be on the team or not in the position they've been asked to play. Team spirit is built by people who are in it for the common good of the team.

5. Shared sufferings.

A healthy team spirit says, "we are in this together"—through good times and hard times. In addition to laughing together, a good-spirited team can cry together through the difficulties of life. Healthy teams are willing to do whatever it takes to accomplish the mission.

6. Shared workload.

There are no turf wars on a healthy team. Silos are eliminated and job descriptions overlap. Everyone pulls equal weight and helps one another accomplish individual and collective goals.

7. Leadership embraces team.

This may be the biggest one. As a leader, it's easy to get distracted with my own responsibilities—even live in my own little world. And let's be honest: some leaders would prefer to lead from the penthouse suite. They give orders well, but do not really enjoy playing the game with the team. A healthy team spirit requires involvement from every level—especially from leadership.

It's a challenge to all leaders—why don't you use this as a checklist of sorts to evaluate how your team is doing? Let's build better teams.

7 CHARACTERISTICS OF A HIGHLY EFFECTIVE LEADERSHIP TEAM MEMBER

The difference between a mediocre employee and a high-performing leader is night and day. A mediocre employee fulfills their job responsibilities and checks off their daily tasks. A highly effective employee takes every project to the next level by asking, "How can we improve this to best meet the needs of the people who will be receiving it?"

Every great leader wants to hire high-capacity team members who are going to take his or her organization to the next level. But how are you supposed to know from a few interviews how effective the candidate will be on your church staff?

Here are six characteristics of a highly effective leader for you to look for when you are interviewing for your next hire:

1. They anticipate the needs of their team.
Highly effective leaders don't sit around until their boss gives them a new project. They ask themselves, "What does my team need, and how can I add value to them today?" They are always trying to think one step

ahead of their team members and anticipate potential roadblocks or challenges the team might face. Instead of sitting back and hoping someone else does the work, they take ownership and make things happen.

2. They bring solutions instead of problems.

Mediocre employees bring attention to a problem. Exceptional employees bring a suggested solution to a problem that comes up. People on the solution side of life are positive and bring invaluable energy to the team.

3. They are accessible and responsive.

Highly effective leaders are accessible. They don't isolate themselves from the team. They make themselves available to increase productivity of the team overall. Additionally, highly effective leaders are responsive. Their teammates can count on them to respond promptly and move projects forward. They understand that communication is the key to successful collaboration.

4. They have a NAP (Non-Anxious Presence).

Highly effective leaders understand the value of a NAP—a non-anxious presence. This doesn't mean that they are laid back or give off a complacent attitude toward their work. It is quite the opposite.

A non-anxious presence means listening to the full story when a team member brings up an issue or problem and reacting with a rational, calculated response instead of an emotional, quick-tempered reaction.

5. They know when they are facing burnout...and proactively seek rest.

Highly effective leaders who are adding value to a team run the risk of burning out. They are likely intrinsically motivated and work for the enjoyment of work, not solely for an external reward like a paycheck. Highly effective leaders pay attention to the warning signs of burnout and take action to rest, schedule a vacation, and come back to work refocused to avoid bringing themselves and the rest of the team down.

6. They have the heart of a servant.

We have the option to approach each day with selfishness or selflessness. Highly effective leaders are selfless. They approach their work with the objective of serving their team well. Leaders who approach their day by answering the question, "How can I serve my team today?" are highly effective because they are helping solve the problems of those around them.

7. They know how to prioritize.

Highly effective team leaders know what projects and tasks are more important than others and act on that knowledge. They are able to assess an overwhelming number of responsibilities and set a timeline for when and how they will be completed.

She, too, became an activist, a founding member of Blacks In Government (BIG), Olympic Sports Professional, founder of Children's Angel Network (CAN) International, U. S. Government Service: Department of Defense (DOD), Military Service, Air Force/Army; NATO – North Atlantic Treaty Organization, Office of International Affairs (OIA), Department of Treasury, Diplomat, Foreign Service, Department of State, Federal Law Enforcement Training Center (FLETC), and founding member of Department of Homeland Security (DHS).

STRONG WOMAN vs. WOMAN OF STRENGTH

A strong woman works out every day to keep her body in shape but a woman of strength kneels in prayer to keep her soul in shape...

A strong woman isn't afraid of anything but a woman of strength shows courage in the midst of her fear...

A strong woman won't let anyone get the best of her but a woman of strength gives the best of herself to everyone...

A strong woman walks sure-footedly but a woman of strength knows God will catch her when she falls...

A strong woman wears the look of confidence on her face but a woman of strength wears her grace...

A strong woman has faith that she is strong enough for the journey but a woman of strength has faith that it is in the journey that she will become strong...

T E A M
TOGETHER
EVERYONE
ACHIEVES
MORE

The Spirit Soul Connection

Trust in HIS timing

Rely on HIS promises

Wait for HIS answer

Believe in HIS miracles

Rejoice in HIS goodness!

Relax in HIS presence

Come near to God and He will come near to you.

(James 4:8)

Happiness keeps us sweet

Trials keep us strong

Sorrow keeps us human!

Failure keeps us humble

God keeps us going.

SPIRITUAL HAPPINESS IS NOT A DESTINATION...IT IS A METHOD OF LIFE

A Letter from HIM

My name is God. You hardly have time for me.

I love you and always bless you. I am always with you.

I need you to spend 10% of your 24 hours with Me today.

Just praise and pray.

We must go through the storm to appreciate the sunshine!

Be the change! Make a difference today. (2 Corinth12:9)

Hebrews 10:35-36 New International Version (NIV)

So do not throw away your confidence; it will be richly rewarded. You need to persevere so that when you have done the will of God, you will receive what he has promised.

(FI) – FELLOWSHIP INTERNATIONAL

Affirms the Lordship of Christ over all aspects of life, acknowledges the Bible as the foundational authority for the development of commitment to high goals, and clarifies the implications of biblical truth for its discipline. By developing servant leaders who value integrity, compassion, and justice in all aspects of Christian life, prepares individuals to serve, not to be served.

A young African-American 10 year old girl, Yvette Raymar, came to Southern California in the 1960's with her father and mother the family was transferred from Washington, D.C. and reassigned to El Toro USMC Marine Base, in Orange County California where she first met Agricultural Labor Activist César Chavez – aka - Uncle CC...whom shared some amazing God given life changing humanitarian adventures in changing the course of history together Yvette Raymar and César Chavez – aka – Uncle CC!

LIFE'S TUG OF WAR

Life can seem ungrateful—and not always kind;
Life can pull at your heartstrings—and play with your
    mind;
Life can be blissful—and happy and free;
Life can put beauty in the things that you see;
Life can place challenges right at your feet;
Life can make good of the hardships we meet;
Life can overwhelm you—and make your head spin;
Life can reward those determined to win;
Life can be hurtful—and not always fair;
Life can surround you with people who care;
Life clearly does offer its Up and its Downs;
Life's days can bring you both smiles and frowns;
Life teaches us to take the good with the bad;
Life is a mixture--- happy and sad—SO...
Take the life that you have and give it your best...
Think positive, be happy—let God do the rest...

Take the challenges that life has laid at your feet;
Take pride and be thankful for each one you meet;
To yourself give forgiveness if you stumble and fall;
Take each day that is dealt you and give it your all;
Take the love that you're given and return it with
    care...
Have faith that when needed—it will always be there...
Take time to find the beauty in the things that you
    see...
Take life's simple pleasures—let them set you free...
The idea here is simple—to even the score—
As you are met and faced with LIFE'S TUG OF WAR.

Character is like a tree and a reputation like a shadow. The shadow is what we think of it; the tree is the real thing... Good actions give strength to ourselves and inspire good actions in others; ability is what you're capable of doing motivation determines what you do. Attitude determines how well you do it.

Unless an individual undertakes more than he possibly can do, they will never do all that they can.

J E W E L S: J = Jubilant E = Emerging W = Woman E = Embracing L = Life S = Seasons

READ THE FIRST PART BY RHONDA DULA:

The Girl Scout Effect: Part I – The Beginning

ASIN: B076JB95QW

Description: Paying tribute to all women who served in the Uniformed Armed Forces, past and present. The Women's Military Forces helped open the way for today's women who serve! Follow this story of a particular Girl Scout, Yvette Raymar, as she takes you through a historical journey as one of the last of the Women's Military Forces, Vietnam and Southeast Asia...

AVAILABLE NOW ON AMAZON.

About Atmosphere Press

Atmosphere Press is an independent, full-service publisher for excellent books in all genres and for all audiences. Learn more about what we do at atmospherepress.com.

We encourage you to check out some of Atmosphere's latest releases, which are available at Amazon.com and via order from your local bookstore:

Love and Asperger's: Jim and Mary's Excellent Adventure, by Mary A. Johnson, Ph.D.

Down, Looking Up, by Connie Rubsamen

Embodying the 12 Steps Workbook: Kundalini Yoga for Recovery, by Rachel Surinderjot Kaur

Home at the Office: Working Remotely as a Way of Life, by Barbori Garnet

God? WTF?!, by Charmaine Loverin

Chasing Corporate Compliance: Why Your Company is Playing Compliance Catch Up!, by John C. Vescera

My Way Forward: Turning Tragedy into Triumph, by Molei Wright

In Pursuit of Calm, by Daniel Fuselier, PsyD

UFOs of the Kickapoo, by John Sime

About the Author

As an author, Rhonda Dula donates the proceeds from 15 of her 20 written books to CAN (Children's Angel Network, Southeast Asia). She is a retired founding member of the Office of International Affairs of the U.S. Department of Homeland Security. Her professional experience includes honorable military; serving in NATO (North Atlantic Treaty Organization) in England, Spain, and Italy as well as Southeast Asia; and going on to serve the United States Department of Treasury and Bureau of U.S. Customs Service as a federal law enforcement officer.

She attributes her hard work towards leaving a legacy to her grandchildren and future generations to come. She received her PhD in Project Management in Organizational

Development in 2003. She is a founding vice president of People Skills International, lifetime founding member of Blacks in Government (BIG), founder of CAN (Children's Angel Network) Human Trafficking Witness Protection Program in Southeast Asia, and Founding Youth President of Orange County California Chapter of the NAACP (National Association Advancement of Colored People).

Links:

https://www.linkedin.com/in/dr-rhonda-dula-95950117
https://www.facebook.com/rhonda.dula
https://www.rhondadula.com

Invisible Project Documentaries:
Dula, Profile Bio: https://youtu.be/c3Ers2ajkTU
Dula, Activist: https://youtu.be/zk8QxtAaxOQ

About the Artist

DeLois Johnson, freelance artist, discovered at an early age that she could make magic with just a pencil and paint brush. Thanks to a keen-eyed third-grade teacher who spotted her artistic abilities, DeLois was encouraged to put her creative talents to work for the school. The talented young artist racked up awards, creating everything from attention-grabbing bulletin boards to bold, colorful floats for the annual school parades.

DeLois spontaneously draws animated cartoon characters on demand. Her favorite pastime is sketching imaginary paper doll models, dressed in fashionable designer couture worthy of a *Vanity Fair* cover. Over the years, DeLois perfected her art skills, studying the craft while taking art classes. She landed a job in the 1980s with

Sears Roebuck and Company as a visual merchandiser, creating window displays for Texas mall stores. Although her career in real estate occupies more of her time, she has never forgotten her passion for art and the magic that comes with it.

Inspired by the author, Dr. Rhonda Dula, PhD, *Uncle CC and Me* gave the opportunity to create a patriotic red, white, and blue book cover accented with gold stars fit for an American hero. Cesar Chavez, an Agricultural Labor Activist, served in the U.S. Navy. He shared an amazing God-given life of adventures, changing the course of history.

DeLois O. Johnson
PO Box 421192
Houston, Texas 77242
deejohnson48@sbcglobal.net
(832) 228-7986

Made in the USA
Middletown, DE
14 March 2022

62497268R00059